# TALL TALES

## 11 Leveled Stories to Read
## Together for Gaining Fluency & Compreh...

by
Kathryn Wheeler
and Debra Olson Pressnall

**Key Education**
Carson-Dellosa Publishing Company LLC
Greensboro, North Carolina

*www.keyeducationpublishing.com*

## CONGRATULATIONS ON YOUR PURCHASE OF A KEY EDUCATION PRODUCT!

The editors at Key Education are former teachers who bring experience, enthusiasm, and quality to each and every product. Thousands of teachers have looked to the staff at Key Education for new and innovative resources to make their work more enjoyable and rewarding. Key Education is committed to developing and publishing educational materials that will assist teachers in building a strong and developmentally appropriate curriculum for young children.

### PLAN FOR GREAT TEACHING EXPERIENCES WHEN YOU USE EDUCATIONAL MATERIALS FROM KEY EDUCATION

## About the Authors

**Kathryn Wheeler** has worked as a teacher, an educational consultant, and an editor in educational publishing. She has published workbooks, stories, and magazine articles for children. Kate was awarded a Michigan Council for the Arts grant for fiction. She has a B.A. degree in English from Hope College. Kate lives in Michigan with her husband, Don.

**Debra Olson Pressnall** has been an editor, writer, and product developer in the educational publishing field for over 20 years. She earned her bachelor of science degree in elementary education from Concordia College (Minnesota) and then spent 12 years as an educator in elementary classrooms before entering the supplemental education publishing field. She has authored dozens of classroom teaching aids as well as 12 books for teachers, including Key Education's *Lively Literacy & Music Activities* and *Sound Out and Sort*. Debra has been the recipient of two Directors' Choice Awards, two *Creative Child Magazine* Awards, and a Parents' Choice Honors award. She lives in Minnesota with her very supportive husband, Steve, and son, Brandon.

## Credits
**Content Editor and Layout Design:** Debra Olson Pressnall
**Copy Editor:** Karen Seberg
**Inside Illustrations:** Julie Anderson
**Cover Design:** Annette Hollister-Papp
**Cover Illustrations:** JJ Rudisill
**Cover Photographs:** © Shutterstock

## Key Education
An imprint of Carson-Dellosa Publishing LLC
PO Box 35665
Greensboro, NC 27425 USA
www.keyeducationpublishing.com

Printed in the USA • All rights reserved.

ISBN 978-1-602681-33-0
01-335118091

# Table of Contents

# Building Fluency & Comprehension Skills with Tall Tales

If your students can decode words and recognize many high-frequency words but read passages word-for-word with monotone voices, there are strategies that can help them become fluent readers. Perhaps you are asking, what is fluency? Is it more than just reading a certain number of words in a passage accurately per minute? When students read aloud effortlessly with expression, comprehension, and accuracy and at a proper rate, they have become fluent readers. Fluency instruction is the bridge from phonics and sight-word practice to comprehension.

In *Partner Read-Alouds: Tall Tales*, familiar and well-loved stories have been retold with simple sentence structures to help struggling and reluctant readers gain fluency. Accompanying each story are comprehension activities to build understanding of story elements. *To find out the readability of each story, which was determined by using the Spache Formula, please refer to the Table of Contents.*

Enjoy these new versions of time-honored folktales as you guide your students down the path toward fluency!

## Strategies for Improving Fluency

- **Select stories that draw students into seeing mental images when reading them.** The genre of tall tales has had an appeal to children for over two centuries. Many of these stories originated when the North American continent seemed huge, frightening, and unknowable. How did pioneers face a world this big and terrifying? They invented larger-than-life characters who were easily a match for the land—as the pioneers themselves would prove to be in time.

  The stories in *Partner Read-Alouds: Tall Tales* engage young readers with main characters who perform incredible feats and are described with figurative language, such as *hyperbole*, or exaggeration.

- **Model for students how to read a passage fluently and how to comprehend while reading.** It is helpful for struggling readers to hear how your voice changes in pitch and conveys emotion, how you pause at the end of sentences, and how you cluster words in meaningful ways. To introduce each story in this resource, have students listen and read along silently while you read aloud the first page. Then, follow up with a discussion: point out punctuation marks in the text, talk about how the tone of your voice conveyed emotion, explain new vocabulary, and so on. This introductory session is also a perfect opportunity to demonstrate how a reader thinks about what is being read. At the appropriate times when rereading the text, think

out loud by posing questions good readers might ask themselves about the passage. And, before allowing students to read the second page, ask them to predict what event might happen next.

- **Have students read aloud the same story several times to polish expressive reading skills and to recognize more words automatically.** These can be large- or small-group choral reading, echo reading, and paired reading experiences. The funny dialogue and repeated thoughts in each story help students gain fluency through expression and repetition within the text as well.

# Maximizing In-Class and Out-of-Class Reading-Aloud Experiences

Keeping students engaged and enjoying the read-aloud sessions is very important. They can lose interest if the same approach is used time after time. So here are some ideas for you to consider:

• **Dramatize Passages with a Theatrical Flair!** Try using different voices for characters as you read aloud a story. There will be lots of smiles in your classroom if you do! And, you might notice children trying their best to be just as dramatic when reading with their partners. It certainly makes the characters come to life!

• **Plan Choral Readings:** Having everyone read at the same time supports those children who are uncomfortable reading aloud. During these sessions, it is important **not** to draw attention to individual children by asking them to read a short passage for the entire class. All of your students must listen carefully to read as "one voice" with you as the leader and not be nervous about the possibility of being singled out to read by themselves.

• **Assign Parts Like a Readers' Theater:** The stories in this book can also be modified easily into a

Readers' Theater script. If available, use interactive white board software and project a copy of a story for the class to read. Work through the story and highlight those parts in yellow that can be handled by a narrator. Assign a reader for that role. Designate small groups of children as Reader 1 or Reader 2. Then, let students "perform" the story using their best theatrical "one voice."

• **Encourage Reading with a Buddy in Class and out of Class:** In addition to what takes place during your guided-reading sessions, it is important for children to read aloud a story with a partner to strengthen their fluency skills. A lot of practice is needed before students can read smoothly and with expression. By having a partner listen to them read designated parts of a story, struggling readers can receive immediate feedback and encouragement. They also sharpen their auditory skills by listening to someone else read as they follow along with the text. The benefit is that students recognize more words automatically and gain awareness of when to pause. *Use the parent letters on page 6 to seek additional support from families.*

# Thinking About Each Story

Boosting reading comprehension skills can be approached in two different ways when using the stories in this book.

**Guided-Reading Sessions:** Introduce a tall tale by reading the first page aloud for students. Then, stop at the end of that page and ask students to predict what they think will happen next. Invite them to discuss their predictions with partners before telling their ideas to the class. This is also a perfect opportunity for students to analyze story elements and explain about what they have learned so far about the main character. Then, record your students' observations about the story on your white board for future discussions. If interested, read aloud the second page to find out if your students' predictions were accurate. Pause occasionally and share your thoughts about the story by "thinking out loud," telling the class any questions you might have. Explain how good readers have a stream of mental questions that are answered as they read a passage.

**Postreading Activities:** Included for each story are two reading activity sheets that target specific comprehension skills. It is recommended that students complete one of the activity pages at the end of each partner read-aloud session. The following skills are addressed through these activities:

• recalling story details

• sequencing story events in proper order

• using vocabulary

• identifying cause-and-effect relationships

• explaining the main character's problem and how it was solved

• identifying the use of hyperbole

• comparing and contrasting characters' traits

• making an inference

• drawing conclusions

• writing a tall tale

Dear Parents,

During the school year, students in your child's class will be reading out loud to improve their reading fluency. Perhaps you are asking, what is fluency? Take a moment to recall your own experiences when you had to read a selection out loud. Did you think about the context of the passage and watched for punctuation marks while conveying emotion with your voice and reading the words in meaningful groupings? This is reading fluency!

At certain times, your child will bring home a tall tale story to share with you. I am inviting you to help your child with this assignment by being a "reading buddy." Please make these reading experiences enjoyable for your child. If your child mispronounces a word while reading aloud, use these strategies:

- Wait to see what your child does before correcting the error.
- Offer clues to help your child figure out the word.
- If the first two strategies are not effective, then tell your child the word.

By having your child read the story aloud several times, the number of words that are recognized automatically will increase. If certain words are troublesome, it is helpful to print the sentences or phrases that contain those words on index cards and have your child practice reading aloud that text separately. Make it fun!

If you have any questions about these reading assignments, please contact me.

Sincerely,

Dear Parents,

In class, your child has been reading aloud the attached story with a partner to become a more fluent reader.

Would you have a few minutes to be your child's "reading buddy"? Let your child choose one of the parts, giving you the remaining role in the script. Then, read the story together out loud. And, for sure, use your most expressive voice to make this storytelling time a pleasant experience and a lot of fun! Repeated readings of the story are always encouraged as well.

Finally, please write a brief message on the back of this paper about the reading session and the progress your child is making. Return this paper by _____.

Thank you for assisting your child with this reading assignment.

Sincerely,


_____ and I have read the story together.


_____
*Parent signature*

# – Teacher's Page –
# Johnny Appleseed and the Animals

## Background

John Chapman was a real person who was born in the 1700s and died in 1845. He walked through the wilderness of what is now Indiana, Illinois, and Ohio, planting trees. Many tales are told about his love of animals.

## Demonstrating Fluent Reading

Model fluent reading for your students by reading aloud the first page. After the reading, ask students to predict what might happen next in the story.

In this story, there are several places where exclamation points indicate surprise, such as, "People laughed at the odd man who would not even ride his own horse!" Explain to your students that this punctuation was used to show the surprise of the onlookers. Read these sentences with dramatic flair to emphasize the feelings in the story.

## Prereading Activity: Building Vocabulary

Before reading the story, review these vocabulary words with your students:

| | | | |
|---|---|---|---|
| cleared | cider | earth | trading post |
| checked | limped | wrapped | odd |
| settlers | ghost | | |

## Reading with a Buddy

Pair students and have them be partners.

**Day 1:** Let students read aloud the story with "one voice" in unison to work on word recognition and fluency skills.

**Day 2:** Direct students to choose a part and read the story aloud again.

**Day 3:** Have students switch parts and reread the story to each other.

At the end of the third day, let your students show off how fluently they can read this story by taking home a copy of it. Encourage each student to read it aloud with a parent or another adult and then return the signed parent letter. (See page 6.)

## Postreading Activities: Comprehension

**Day 1:** After they read the script aloud with partners, have the student pairs discuss what they liked about the story. You may wish to have students underline words in the story that are examples of *hyperbole*, or exaggeration.

**Day 2:** Let students complete the crossword puzzle activity on page 10.

**Day 3:** Direct students to complete the activity Thinking About the Story on page 11 by analyzing Johnny Appleseed's actions, the problem Johnny faced, and how he felt about animals.

## Character Education Connection

Discuss the idea of kind treatment of animals.
- What does it mean to tame an animal?
- Is it better to teach an animal by scaring it or by being kind? Why?
- What did Johnny's actions show about his feelings for animals?

## Language Connection

Ask students to pretend Brother Wolf is talking to Johnny. Students can brainstorm dialogue together. Then, have them try to write down the words the characters say.

# Johnny Appleseed and the Animals

**Reader 1** "May I have these apple seeds?" asked the man. He was wearing a pot on his head.

**Reader 2** "They are no good to us," said the man at the mill. "Take them."

**Reader 1** The man was Johnny Appleseed. Early in his life, he had an idea. He would walk all over the new land that people cleared. They needed apple trees. Johnny loved apples. So he planted trees wherever he went.

**Reader 2** He got his seeds for free. He would go to mills where people made cider. He took the seeds that were left over. He dried them out. Then, they were good for planting. Johnny gave seeds away to people heading west. And, he also planted trees as he walked.

**Reader 1** Johnny liked to feel the earth under his feet. So he never wore shoes. He liked to keep his hands free for planting. So he wore his cooking pot on his head. He had no money. So he wore old sacks for clothes. Johnny may have looked odd to people. But, animals loved him.

**Reader 2** Everywhere that Johnny went, animals would flock around him. Birds would sit on his finger and sing to him. Rabbits would hop right up to him. The animals knew they could trust Johnny.

**Reader 1** One day, Johnny came to a trading post. Outside was a poor, old horse. The horse had not been treated well. Its head hung down low. It looked sad and dirty. Johnny patted the horse. Then, he went inside the store.

**Reader 2** "What can I do for you, friend?" asked the clerk.

**Reader 1** "I have some good seeds," said Johnny. "I would like to trade them for that horse outside."

**Reader 2** "That old horse?" asked the clerk. "Someone just left her here. She's no good for anything!"

**Reader 1** "I want the trade," said Johnny. He handed over his seeds. He untied the horse. The horse limped behind him to the woods. Johnny found a stream. He let the horse drink. Then, Johnny spent all day washing and brushing her. He checked her feet. He dug out stones from each hoof. After that, he let the horse rest. They spent many days together in the sun. The horse got better. Johnny named the horse Jenny.

**Reader 2** Johnny and Jenny started off walking again. Johnny never rode Jenny. She got too tired if he did. So Johnny just led her on a rope. People laughed at the odd man who would not even ride his own horse!

**Reader 1** One day, Johnny heard an animal crying in the woods. He found a huge wolf. Its leg was caught in a big, steel trap. The wolf looked at Johnny and did not growl. It did not try to bite Johnny. The wolf knew that Johnny would help it.

**Reader 2** Johnny got the wolf out of the trap. He wrapped the wolf's hurt leg in cloth. Once again, Johnny set up camp. He and Jenny waited until the wolf was better.

**Reader 1** Then, they started off again. But, the wolf would not go back to the woods. It followed Johnny like a huge dog! Johnny named him Brother Wolf.

**Reader 2** The settlers got to know Johnny. They would look for the man wearing his cooking pot as a hat. They would see him leading an old horse. And, they would see a gray wolf following him. People grew to love Johnny. Sometimes, he would stay for a meal. Sometimes, he would sleep in a barn. But he walked on, planting seeds. Johnny took care of the little trees until they grew big and full of round, red apples.

**Reader 1** Some people say you can still see the ghost of Johnny walking among the apple trees at night. Jenny and Brother Wolf are by his side.

Name: _____

## Johnny Appleseed and the Animals:
## Checking for Details

**Word Bank**

| apples | limped | settlers |
|--------|--------|----------|
| cider | post | shoes |
| earth | pot | stones |
| ghost | sacks | wolf |
| horse | seeds | |

**Across**

2. The _____ was caught in a trap.
4. Johnny wore a _____ on his head.
7. He liked to feel the _____ under his feet.
8. Johnny didn't wear _____ on his feet.
11. The new people who cleared the land were called _____.
12. Apples were used to make _____.
13. Johnny dug out _____ from Jenny's hoof.

**Down**

1. Johnny liked to eat _____.
3. At first, Jenny _____ as she walked.
5. Johnny stopped at a store called a trading _____.
6. Some people say that you can still see the _____ of Johnny walking among apple trees.
9. Jenny was a _____.
10. Johnny wore old _____ for clothes.
11. Apple _____ were planted by Johnny.

 *Partner Read-Alouds: Tall Tales*

Name: _____

# Johnny Appleseed and the Animals: Thinking About the Story

**Directions:** A **cause** makes something happen. An **effect** happens as a result of a cause. Write the cause or effect in the blank.

| Cause | | Effect |
|-------|---|--------|

**1.** Johnny took apple seeds left at the mills and dried them.  ➡  _____  _____

**2.** Johnny released the wolf's leg from the trap.  ➡  _____  _____

**3.** _____  _____  ➡  The apple trees grew big and produced fruit.

**Directions:** Use sentences to answer the questions.

**1.** What was the wolf's problem that Johnny solved

_____

_____

_____

_____

**2.** How did Johnny feel about animals? What actions showed these feelings? Explain your answer on another sheet of paper.

## – Teacher's Page –
# Bess Call

## Background
This story is based on the tall tales of Joe Call, a farmer from upstate New York who was the strongest man alive. His sister, Bess, was no slouch either, as this story shows.

## Demonstrating Fluent Reading

Model fluent reading for your students by reading aloud the first page. After the reading, ask students to predict what might happen next in the story.

Help students with fluency by having them read several parts of the story more than once. They can use the dialogue to make this more interesting by adding different emphasis to a line each time.

Instruct students to listen as you read the following line: "'Wrestle with me, Joe,' the man would cry." Then, repeat the lines as "Wrestle with me, Joe?" and "Wrestle with me, Joe!" Ask how each one is different. Invite individual students to read dialogue lines with different emphasis and then talk as a class about the meaning that each inflection adds.

## Prereading Activity: Building Vocabulary

Before reading the story, review these vocabulary words with your students:

| | | | |
|---|---|---|---|
| wrestling | horseshoe | stranger | joking |
| practice | match | mountains | plopped |

Be sure to point out the 19th century expressions, such as "sit a spell" and "feeling poorly."

## Reading with a Buddy

Pair students and have them be partners.

**Day 1:** Let students read aloud the story with "one voice" in unison to work on word recognition and fluency skills.

**Day 2:** Direct students to choose a part and read the story aloud again.

**Day 3:** Have students switch parts and reread the story to each other.

At the end of the third day, let your students show off how fluently they can read this story by taking home a copy of it. Encourage each student to read it aloud with a parent or another adult and then return the signed parent letter. (See page 6.)

## Postreading Activities: Comprehension

**Day 1:** After they read the script aloud with partners, have the student pairs discuss what they liked about the story. You may wish to have students underline words in the story that are examples of *hyperbole*, or exaggeration.

**Day 2:** Let students complete the comparing and contrasting activity on page 15.

**Day 3:** Direct students to complete the activity Thinking About the Story on page 16 by analyzing the main character Bess Call and the problem she faced and by making inferences about the stranger and Joe.

## Character Education Connection:
Discuss the idea of equality.
- Are girls able to do things as well as boys?
- What mistake did the stranger make about Bess?
- Why was Bess angry when the stranger laughed at her?

## Language Arts Connection:
Read another story about an amazing woodswoman. One great example is *Swamp Angel* by Anne Isaacs. In this story a strong, powerful woman also gets into a wrestling match—this time with a bear.

## – The Tall Tale –

# Bess Call

**Reader 1** Now, Joe Call was a strong man. Some said he was the strongest man alive. But, Joe was tired of wrestling. Every day another man would come to his farm. "Wrestle with me, Joe!" the man would cry. Joe would sigh. He had chores to do.

**Reader 2** Joe shared his farm. He had a sister named Bess. She was pretty. Bess had blue eyes and black hair. She was tall and strong. But, folks did not know just how strong she was. Bess worked hard on the farm.

**Reader 2** One hot day, she said to Joe, "Let's sit a spell on the porch. I'm all tuckered out."

**Reader 1** She and Joe sat and rocked. A stranger walked up the road. "Are you Joe Call?" he asked.

**Reader 2** Joe nodded. "Sure am," he said.

**Reader 1** "I have come all the way from England. Do you know why?"

**Reader 2** "Can't say that I do," said Joe.

**Reader 1** "To wrestle with you!" said the stranger.

**Reader 2** Joe shook his head. "I'm too tired tonight," he said.

**Reader 1** "I'll be back," said the stranger.

**Reader 2** Joe sighed. He shook his head again. Bess said, "Don't you worry none. When that stranger comes back, I'll fix things."

**Reader 2** The next day, Joe went to town. He needed to trade some eggs for some nails. Bess was out in the barn. She had a horseshoe in her hand.

**Reader 1** "Is your brother home?" asked the stranger.

**Reader 2** "He is not," said Bess.

**Reader 1** "I wanted to wrestle with him," said the stranger.

**Reader 2** "Well, now," said Bess. "Why don't you ask me to wrestle?"

**Reader 2** The stranger laughed. He thought Bess was joking. Bess looked at the man. Her eyes looked angry. She said, "If you can throw me, maybe you are good enough to wrestle with Joe."

**Reader 1** The stranger laughed harder. He could not believe it. A lady was asking him to wrestle.

**Reader 2** Now, Bess was really mad. She took that iron horseshoe and bent it in her hands. Then, she tied it in a knot. "So you think I'm not good enough because I'm a girl?" she asked.

**Reader 1** The stranger said, "Well, maybe I could wrestle you for practice."

**Reader 2** Bess rolled up her sleeves. She and the stranger started to wrestle. They rolled all the way to the mountains. Then, they rolled back down to the farm. The dust from the match blocked out the sun. People miles away could hear Bess shouting and yelling as the match went on.

**Reader 2** Bess and the stranger wrestled from morning to night. The match ended when Bess picked up the man by his pants. She lifted him up in the air. She plopped him on the other side of the gate. "I win," she said.

**Reader 1** "What about my horse?" asked the stranger.

**Reader 2** "Oh, yes," said Bess. She walked over to the barn. She picked up the man's horse. She lifted it over the fence. "There you go!" said Bess.

**Reader 1** The stranger got on his horse. He rode away as fast as he could.

**Reader 1** Later, Joe came home. "Was that the stranger from England I saw riding off?" he asked.

**Reader 2** "It was," said Bess.

**Reader 1** "Did you win?" asked Joe.

**Reader 2** "Yes, I did," said Bess. "And I didn't have the heart to tell him that I am feeling poorly today, too."

Name: _____

# Bess Call: Comparing and Contrasting Characters

**Directions:** Read the words in the boxes below. Which words tell about Bess? Which words tell about the stranger? Which words tell about both people? Cut out the words. Glue each one in the correct section of the Venn diagram.

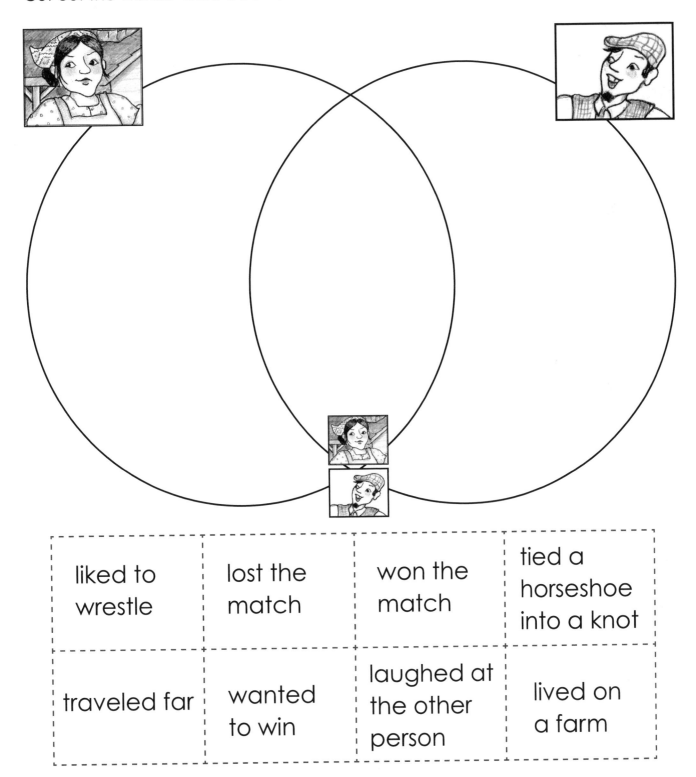

| liked to wrestle | lost the match | won the match | tied a horseshoe into a knot |
| traveled far | wanted to win | laughed at the other person | lived on a farm |

# Bess Call: Thinking About the Story

**Directions:** Look at the pictures. Use sentences to answer the questions.

**1.** What do you think Bess was thinking?

**2.** What do you think the stranger was thinking?

_____ 

_____

_____ 

_____

**3.** What was Bess's problem in the story?

_____

_____

**Draw a Conclusion.** How did Joe feel when he did not have to wrestle the stranger? Explain your answer.

_____

_____

_____

# – Teacher's Page –
# Annie and the Storm

## Background

This story is based on tales of Annie Christmas, a fictional character who first appeared in print in 1945, although oral tales of her are much older. This giant of a character lived in New Orleans and was a boat pilot on the Mississippi River.

## Demonstrating Fluent Reading

Model fluent reading for your students by reading aloud the first page. After the reading, ask students to predict what might happen next in the story.

Be sure to discuss the text with **bold italics**; this tale was written deliberately to have sections with special emphasis. Show students how a bold, italicized word gets the most emphasis.

Ask students, "Did you hear how I read the two lines, 'Go away! This is my boat!'? My voice got louder when I said *my*. That is because the captain is saying, 'This isn't your boat! It's mine!'" Point out to students that they may hear this emphasis all the time from younger siblings.

## Prereading Activity: Building Vocabulary

Before reading the story, review these vocabulary words with your students:

| | | | |
|---|---|---|---|
| pounds | keelboat | steer | barrels |
| riverboat | hotel | dock | waist |

## Reading with a Buddy

Pair students and have them be partners.

**Day 1:** Let students read aloud the story with "one voice" in unison to work on word recognition and fluency skills.

**Day 2:** Direct students to choose a part and read the story aloud again.

**Day 3:** Have students switch parts and reread the story to each other.

At the end of the third day, let your students show off how fluently they can read this story by taking home a copy of it. Encourage each student to read it aloud with a parent or another adult and then return the signed parent letter. (See page 6.)

## Postreading Activities: Comprehension

**Day 1:** After they read the script aloud with partners, have the student pairs discuss what they liked about the story. You may wish to have students underline words in the story that are examples of *hyperbole*, or exaggeration.

**Day 2:** Let students complete the comprehension activity and word search on page 20.

**Day 3:** Direct students to complete the activity Thinking About the Story on page 21 by analyzing the main character Annie Christmas, her traits, and the problem Annie faced.

## Character Education Connection

Discuss the idea of equality.

- Why did people used to think that women could not do things as well as men?
- What job would you like to have when you grow up?
- How would you feel if someone told you that you could not have a certain job because you were male or female?

## Social Studies Connection

Show pictures of riverboats to your students. Talk about life on the Mississippi River in the 19th century.

# Annie and the Storm

**Reader 1** The big river was strong. But Annie Christmas was stronger. Annie was six feet eight inches tall. She weighed 300 pounds. She had beautiful black skin. She had long black hair. She had eyes like stars. She was the only woman on the big river who had her own keelboat.

**Reader 2** A keelboat is a big, flat boat. It carries food and people up and down the river. Annie could steer her boat all by herself. She could carry things on and off all by herself. In fact, she could carry three barrels at the same time—one under each arm and one on her head.

**Reader 1** Annie had 12 sons. Each one had been born on December 25. Each one was seven feet tall. Annie's sons all worked on the river, too. But, Annie never asked them for help. She liked doing things herself.

**Reader 2** One day, Annie said, "Goodness sakes! I haven't had a day off since I don't know when. It's time for me to have some **fun**."

**Reader 1** So Annie put on her red dress. She put red feathers in her hair. She steered her boat over to a big riverboat called the *Belle*. She tied her boat behind the *Belle* and climbed on board.

**Reader 2** A riverboat is like a floating hotel. People had rooms on the boat. There were places to eat. People played cards. Annie had a fine time.

**Reader 1** That night, a big storm came. The wind was strong. The rain was heavy. The captain of the *Belle* had trouble steering the big boat. Annie could see that the riverboat was headed for a sandbar. Then, they would be in big trouble. The boat could tip over. The people inside could die. Annie ran to the captain and said, "Let **me** take that wheel. I will get this boat out of trouble!"

**Reader 2** The captain said, "Go away! This is **my** boat! I will steer this boat the way I see fit."

**Reader 1** The rain and the wind got worse. The big river was filled with huge waves. Annie could see trees in the water. If the *Belle* hit a tree, the boat could sink. She ran to the captain again. "Let me help!" said Annie. "I know this river better than you do!"

**Reader 2** The captain said, "You are only a woman. Go away!"

**Reader 1** Well, that made Annie mad. She went to the side of the boat where her own keelboat was tied. She pulled the boats close together. Then, she jumped on board.

**Reader 1** "If anybody wants to come with me, jump now!" Annie yelled. "You will be safer with me!"

**Reader 2** Now, a riverboat is a big boat. A keelboat is much smaller. In a storm, it seemed like the riverboat would be safer. But the people on the *Belle* knew that Annie was strong and brave. And, they knew she could help them. So, they all jumped on board.

**Reader 1** "Right!" said Annie. She handed out poles. "Let's get this boat turned around."

**Reader 2** Everybody worked together. They turned the keelboat. Annie steered the boat close to shore. She quickly jumped off onto land with a rope.

**Reader 1** "I'll get you all back home again!" Annie said. She tied that rope around her waist. Then, she pulled that boat back to the city all by herself. She ran the whole way. The boat felt like it was flying.

**Reader 2** "Hooray for Annie Christmas!" the people shouted. "She saved our lives!" Her 12 sons came down to the dock. They hugged their mother. Later, everyone found out that the *Belle* **did** hit a sandbar. It **did** tip over on one side. The captain got to shore. Nobody would ever let that man steer a boat on the big river again.

# Annie and the Storm: Checking for Details

**Directions:** Read each sentence about the story. Write a "**T**" on the blank if the sentence is true. Write an "**F**" on the blank if the sentence is false.

**1.** Annie could carry three barrels at a time.                    _____

**2.** Annie's sons worked on her keelboat.                    _____

**3.** The keelboat carried goods and people up and down
    the river.                    _____

**4.** Annie had seven sons who were each 12 feet tall.                    _____

**5.** The storm caused huge waves on the river.                    _____

**6.** People stay in rooms and eat food on a riverboat.                    _____

**7.** During the storm, Annie helped the captain steer the
    riverboat.

**Directions:** Read the words in the Word Bank. Circle them in the word find.

**Word Bank**

barrels
captain
dock
hotel
jump
keelboat
pounds
rain
steer
storm
waist
wheel

| c | t | p | o | u | n | d | s |
|---|---|---|---|---|---|---|---|
| a | w | a | i | s | t | h | x |
| p | z | o | v | t | c | o | j |
| t | x | b | w | o | r | t | u |
| a | b | a | h | r | a | e | m |
| i | s | r | e | m | i | l | p |
| n | t | r | e | t | n | v | w |
| k | e | e | l | b | o | a | t |
| d | e | l | q | b | w | o | l |
| q | r | s | p | d | o | c | k |

Name: _____

# Annie and the Storm: Thinking About the Story

**Directions:** Use sentences to answer the questions.

**1.** Underline the words in the story that tell how strong Annie was. Why is this an exaggeration? Illustrate a picture about Annie.

_____

_____

**2.** What was Annie's problem in the story?

_____

_____

**3.** Describe how Annie felt when she said, "I'll get you all back home again!"

_____

_____

**Try This!** Would you like to steer a keelboat on the Mississippi River? Explain your answer on another sheet of paper.

# – Teacher's Page –
# Widowmaker

## Background
This story is based on the tall tales from the Old West about Pecos Bill. As the archetypal cowboy, Pecos Bill embodied all of the skills that a cowboy needed to survive.

## Reading with a Buddy
Pair students and have them be partners.

**Day 1:** Let students read aloud the story with "one voice" in unison to work on word recognition and fluency skills.

**Day 2:** Direct students to choose a part and read the story aloud again.

**Day 3:** Have students switch parts and reread the story to each other.

At the end of the third day, let your students show off how fluently they can read this story by taking home a copy of it. Encourage each student to read it aloud with a parent or another adult and then return the signed parent letter. (See page 6.)

## Postreading Activities: Comprehension
**Day 1:** After they read the script aloud with partners, have the student pairs discuss what they liked about the story. You may wish to have students underline words in the story that are examples of *hyperbole*, or exaggeration.

**Day 2:** Let students complete the crossword puzzle on page 25.

**Day 3:** Direct students to complete the activity Thinking About the Story on page 26 by analyzing the problem Pecos Bill faced and how he cared for Widowmaker.

## Demonstrating Fluent Reading
Model fluent reading for your students by reading aloud the first page. After the reading, ask students to predict what might happen next in the story.

It may be helpful to talk about a dialogue section with students. Use part of the talk between Bill and the rancher. Ask students, "Did you hear how I dropped my voice for the words *asked Bill*? That's because these words are not part of what the characters said out loud—it just tells us who was talking."

Point out to your students that your voice is more expressive when you are reading the actual dialogue. Pair students and have them practice reading just the dialogue out loud.

## Character Education Connection
Discuss the idea of talent.
* Are you good at something that nobody else in your family can do?
* What does it mean to have talent? What are some examples of talents?
* How did Pecos Bill's talents help him do his job as a cowboy?

## Arts Connection
Do a play version of "Widowmaker." In addition to the speaking parts, have other students create sound effects. For example, one group of students can be coyote pups and howl in the background! Perform your play for a kindergarten class.

## Prereading Activity: Building Vocabulary
Before reading the story, review these vocabulary words with your students:

| | | | |
|---|---|---|---|
| coyote | lasso | cactus | range |
| twister | yahoo | bucked | Widowmaker |

Be sure also to point out the 19th century expressions, such as "a piece" and "over yonder."

## – The Tall Tale –
# Widowmaker

**Reader 1** Pecos Bill wasn't raised by a human family. When he was just a baby, he fell out of a wagon on its way west. A coyote found him. She sniffed him all over. She picked him up by his neck. She took him back to her den. Bill was raised with a whole family of wild coyote pups.

**Reader 2** Bill could not live with the coyotes forever. So he stood up one day and got himself a job as a cowboy. Bill had to learn many things. But, being a cowboy was easy for him. He could ride wild horses. He could tie up a baby calf faster than anybody. But, what he really loved was roping.

**Reader 1** Bill would hold his lasso. He would swing it around and around. He could rope anything you told him to. It might be a cactus. It might be a whole barn. It did not matter. Pecos Bill was the greatest roper ever.

**Reader 2** Now, one day, he was out on the range with the rest of the cowboys. They were herding cows on the range. They looked up at the sky. It was black!

**Reader 1** "Look over yonder!" shouted one cowboy. There was a twister! The big storm roared like a lion. It was coming straight at the herd.

**Reader 2** "Oh, no, you don't!" shouted Bill. He got out his lasso. He swung that rope around and around. Then, he roped the twister. He leaped off his horse and onto that big storm. It spun around. But, Bill did not fall off. "Yahoo!" he yelled. "This is better than any wild horse around!" And, he rode that storm clean into Texas.

**Reader 2** When that storm finally slowed down, Bill jumped off the twister's back. He looked around. "This is a fine place," he said. "I might stay here a piece."

**Reader 1** Everybody knew that Bill had ridden into Texas on a twister. Everybody wanted to give Bill a job.

**Reader 1** Bill went to work on a ranch. The man who owned the ranch had a whole herd of horses. "Pick any one you want," said the man.

**Reader 2** Bill looked at them all. Then, he saw another horse. It was in a pen all by itself. "What about that horse?" asked Bill.

**Reader 1** "Oh, no," said the rancher. "You don't want that horse. Nobody has ever been able to ride him. We call him Widowmaker."

**Reader 2** "Sounds like just the horse for me!" said Bill. He went over to the pen. Widowmaker stamped his feet. He was a huge, white horse. His eyes were red. Bill said, "Let's you and me go for a ride!"

**Reader 1** Widowmaker squealed in anger. Bill jumped on Widowmaker's back. That horse ran clean across Texas. He bucked. He leaped. He kicked. He did everything he could to throw Bill off of his back. But, Bill had ridden a twister. A horse was no problem at all.

**Reader 2** "Yahoo!" yelled Bill. He was having a great time.

**Reader 1** Bill and Widowmaker rode back and forth across Texas for two whole weeks. At last, Widowmaker got tired. He stopped. He snorted. He hung his head. Bill led him to the barn. He gave Widowmaker a big bucket of water to drink. He gave him oats to eat. He rubbed him down. He patted his head.

**Reader 2** "Don't you feel bad. You are still the roughest, toughest horse in Texas," said Bill. "And, I am going to make you a promise. Nobody will ever ride you except me."

**Reader 1** Widowmaker tossed his head. It was as if he was nodding. It was a deal. Only the roughest, toughest cowboy could ride the roughest, toughest horse. From that day on, Bill and Widowmaker were always together. They rode all over Texas. Everybody knew the great cowboy and his fierce white horse.

Name:

# Widowmaker: Checking for Details

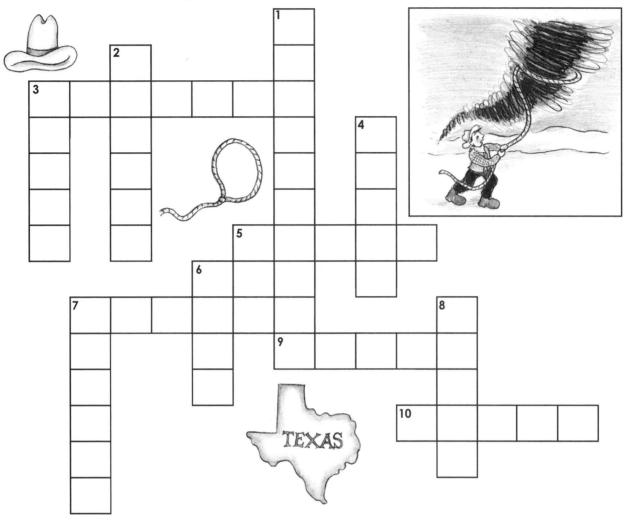

## Word Bank

cactus      rode
cowboy    stamped
coyote     swing
horse      Texas
lasso      Widowmaker
ranch
range

## Across

**3.** When Bill first saw the horse, it _____ its feet.
**5.** Bill used a _____ to rope the twister.
**7.** When he was young, Bill lived like a _____.
**9.** Cowboys herd cows on the _____.
**10.** Bill worked on a _____ in Texas.

## Down

**1.** The name of the horse is _____.
**2.** A _____ is a desert plant.
**3.** Bill would _____ the rope above his head.
**4.** Only Bill would ride his _____ .
**6.** Bill _____ the twister until it slowed down.
**7.** On the ranch, Bill worked as a _____.
**8.** The twister carried Bill into _____.

# Widowmaker:  Thinking About the Story

**Directions:**  Use sentences to answer the questions.

**1.** What could Bill do with a lasso? Draw a picture and explain why this is an exaggeration.

_____

_____

_____

**2.** What was Bill's problem in the story?

_____

_____

**3.** How did Bill care for Widowmaker?

_____

_____

**Try This!**  Would you like to ride a horse like Widowmaker?  Explain your answer on another sheet of paper.

# – Teacher's Page –
# Pecos Bill Gets Married

## Background
This story is based on the tall tale of how Pecos Bill met his bride, Slue-Foot Sue, an adventure-chasing cowgirl.

## Demonstrating Fluent Reading
Model fluent reading for your students by reading aloud the first page. After the reading, ask students to predict what might happen next in the story.

It may be helpful to show students how to voice the first paragraph that explains something. Ask students, "Did you hear how my voice went up on the words *a red-haired woman* when I read, 'And, riding on the back of the fish was a red-haired woman'? That is because this is the biggest surprise in the first paragraph!"

Also, point out the other details in the first paragraph. Discuss with students how expression helps people "see" what the author is describing.

## Prereading Activity: Building Vocabulary
Before reading the story, review these vocabulary words with your students:

| | | | |
|---|---|---|---|
| catfish | howled | promise | wedding |
| fried | Big Dipper | whistled | saddle |

## Reading with a Buddy
Pair students and have them be partners.

**Day 1:** Let students read aloud the story with "one voice" in unison to work on word recognition and fluency skills.

**Day 2:** Direct students to choose a part and read the story aloud again.

**Day 3:** Have students switch parts and reread the story to each other.

At the end of the third day, let your students show off how fluently they can read this story by taking home a copy of it. Encourage each student to read it aloud with a parent or another adult and then return the signed parent letter. (See page 6.)

## Postreading Activities: Comprehension
**Day 1:** After they read the script aloud with partners, have the student pairs discuss what they liked about the story. You may wish to have students underline words in the story that are examples of *hyperbole*, or exaggeration.

**Day 2:** Let students complete the vocabulary and sequencing activity on page 30.

**Day 3:** Direct students to complete the activity Thinking About the Story on page 31 by analyzing the problem Pecos Bill faced and by making an inference about the character.

## Character Education Connection:
Discuss the idea of promises.
- What does it mean to make a promise?
- Has anybody ever broken a promise made to you? What happened?
- Why was Widowmaker angry when Bill broke his promise?

## Science Connection:
Show students a map of the stars. Find the Big Dipper. Talk about other legends and tales that relate to this constellation.

# Pecos Bill Gets Married

**Reader 1** Bill was riding the range on his horse, Widowmaker. It was a beautiful day. He was riding along the Pecos River. Bill gazed at the river. "Look over there!" he said to Widowmaker. There was the biggest catfish that either of them had ever seen. It jumped into the air. It flipped around. It twisted and turned. And, riding on the back of the fish was a red-haired woman.

**Reader 2** "Yahoo!" the woman yelled. The catfish did a back flip. The woman stayed right on that big fish's back.

**Reader 1** "What's your name?" Bill yelled.

**Reader 2** "Why, I'm Slue-Foot Sue!" the woman yelled back. Then, that big catfish went racing down the river. Sue and the fish were gone.

**Reader 1** Bill could not get Slue-Foot Sue out of his mind. That night, he sat looking at the moon. He was thinking about Sue. He howled like a coyote.

**Reader 1** "Yip-yip-yip!" howled Bill.

**Reader 2** Sue stood outside of her cabin. She could hear Bill howl. She knew that Bill was in love with her. She smiled.

**Reader 1** The next day, Bill came over. He carried a bunch of flowers. "Sue, I just have to marry you," said Bill.

**Reader 2** Sue took the flowers. She said, "I will marry you. But, you have to promise me one thing."

**Reader 1** "Anything," said Bill.

**Reader 2** "I want to ride your horse," said Sue.

**Reader 1** Bill smiled. "You can't do that," he said. "Widowmaker won't let anybody but me ride him."

**Reader 2** "I rode that catfish. Do you think that fish wanted me to ride it?" asked Sue.

**Reader 1** Bill said, "But, I promised Widowmaker that nobody would ever ride him except me."

**Reader 2** "Then, I guess we won't get married," said Sue.

**Reader 1** Bill felt awful. He wanted to marry Sue more than anything. So he told Sue that she could ride Widowmaker just one time. Sue said she would ride the big white horse on their wedding day.

**Reader 2** Bill thought that maybe Sue would forget all about it. But right after the wedding, Sue strode outside in her white dress. She put a saddle on Widowmaker's back. Then, she jumped up on the huge horse.

**Reader 2** Widowmaker was mad. He knew that Bill had broken his promise. He bucked. He kicked hard. He raced back and forth. He did back flips. All of a sudden, Sue let go of the reins. Widowmaker kicked so hard that Sue flew all of the way over the moon! Bill had to move quickly. He roped her with his lasso to get her back again.

**Reader 1** That summer, Texas did not get any rain. Everything was hot and dry. Snakes fainted. Hens laid fried eggs. Sheep turned into balls of dust. People came to Bill and asked for his help. "We need rain here, but I don't know what to do," he told Sue.

**Reader 2** Sue replied, "I have an idea. When I flew over the moon, I saw the Big Dipper in the sky. It was full of water. If we lasso that old Big Dipper and pull it down, all of that water will pour down as rain."

**Reader 1** Bill thought that was a fine idea. So he and Sue climbed a big hill. Then, Bill roped the Big Dipper. He whistled for Widowmaker. He tied the rope to Widowmaker's saddle. "Pull, boy!" shouted Bill. Widowmaker pulled and pulled and pulled. Finally, water started to pour down. That night, it rained all over Texas.

Name: _____

**Directions:** Use the vocabulary to complete the sentences.

| **Vocabulary:** | back | bucked | catfish | howled |
|---|---|---|---|---|
| marry | moon | rain | ride | roped | saddle |
| Slue-Foot Sue | water | Widowmaker | | |

One day, Bill was riding _____ along the Pecos River.

In the water was the biggest _____ Bill had ever seen. And, riding on the back of the fish was _____.

That night, Bill thought about Sue. He _____ like a coyote at the _____.

Sue agreed to _____ Bill if she could _____ Widowmaker.

After the wedding, Sue put a _____ on the horse and then jumped on his _____.

Widowmaker _____ so hard that Sue flew over the moon.

Using his lasso, Bill _____ Sue to get her back again.

Sue told Bill about the _____ in the Big Dipper. So he roped it to bring _____ to Texas.

**Try This!** Cut out the sentences and mix them up. Paste them in order on a sheet of paper so that they tell the story.

# Pecos Bill Gets Married: Thinking About the Story

**Directions:** Use sentences to answer the questions.

**1.** What was Slue-Foot Sue's talent? Draw a picture and
explain why this is an exaggeration.

_____

_____

_____

_____

**2.** What was Bill's first problem in the story?

_____

_____

**3.** What words did the author use to tell you about how hot and dry it was in
Texas?  Write one of the ways.

_____

_____

**4.** How did Bill feel after the rain fell?  Explain your answer.

_____

_____

**Tell a Yarn About Bill and Slue-Foot Sue!**  What adventure could the Crocketts
have next?  Write your tall tale on another sheet of paper.

# – Teacher's Page –
# The Dancing Bear

## Background
This tale about Sally Ann Thunder Ann Whirlwind takes place before she met and married the fictional Davy Crockett. Sally Ann was a powerful woman, as many pioneer women were. She was not only strong and hardworking but was clever enough to outsmart both people and animals in order to get herself out of danger.

## Demonstrating Fluent Reading

Model fluent reading for your students by reading aloud the first page. After the reading, ask students to predict what might happen next in the story.

To demonstrate a rhyming section, use Sally Ann's song from the story. Ask students, "Did you hear how I grouped the words 'Round and round and round we go!'? That is because those words are a whole thought that belong together. Then, I paused before I read, 'Dancing fast!'"

For more fluency practice, write the words to Sally Ann's song on the board. Then, have students sing to the tune of "Jack and Jill." (You will have to modify the rhythm of the song slightly to make the lyrics fit.) Singing will help students group the words correctly.

## Prereading Activity: Building Vocabulary

Before reading the story, review these vocabulary words with your students:

| | | | |
|---|---|---|---|
| Whirlwind | powerful | danger | churn |
| dumpling | bowed | weakness | sawed |

Be sure also to point out the 19th century expressions, such as "a good lick of work" and "just fine."

## Reading with a Buddy

Pair students and have them be partners.

**Day 1:** Let students read aloud the story with "one voice" in unison to work on word recognition and fluency skills.

**Day 2:** Direct students to choose a part and read the story aloud again.

**Day 3:** Have students switch parts and reread the story to each other.

At the end of the third day, let your students show off how fluently they can read this story by taking home a copy of it. Encourage each student to read it aloud with a parent or another adult and then return the signed parent letter. (See page 6.)

## Postreading Activities: Comprehension

**Day 1:** After they read the script aloud with partners, have the student pairs discuss what they liked about the story. You may wish to have students underline words in the story that are examples of *hyperbole*, or exaggeration.

**Day 2:** Let students complete the vocabulary activity on page 35.

**Day 3:** Direct students to complete the activity Thinking About the Story on page 36 by analyzing the main character Sally Ann Thunder Ann Whirlwind, her character traits, and the problem she faced.

## Character Education Connection

Discuss the idea of pioneer women.
- What things did pioneer women have to do well?
- What was Sally Ann's most important quality that helped her in this story?
- Make a list of traits that would be good to have if you lived in the wilderness.

## Math Connection

Create simple word problems using Sally's chores in "The Dancing Bear." For example, "If Sally Ann pulled up two trees in one minute, how many could she pull up in thirty minutes?"

## – The Tall Tale –
# The Dancing Bear

**Reader 1** Sally Ann Thunder Ann Whirlwind lived in the big woods. She was fast. She could run up a steep mountain in two seconds flat. She was strong. She could crack nuts open with her teeth. She was powerful. She could rip tall trees out of the ground when she wanted wood for her fire.

**Reader 2** Sally Ann was also smart. She could think her way out of danger. This was the best help she had out in the big woods.

**Reader 1** One day, Sally Ann was working in her cabin. She had been up since dawn. She had carried 200 trees to her yard for firewood. She had dug up 500 rocks from her field. She had planted sweet corn and beans and had watered them. Now, she was preparing a fine meal.

**Reader 2** Sally Ann made stew and dumplings in a big pot and set it on a roaring fire to cook. Then, she went outside to do more chores. While making butter in a churn, she looked up and saw a huge bear. The animal was lumbering right up to Sally Ann's cabin!

**Reader 1** "Tarnation!" said Sally Ann. She whirled into her cabin. She grabbed a dumpling from the pot. When the bear walked in, she quickly stuffed that dumpling into his big mouth.

**Reader 2** The bear chewed. He smiled. It was the best dumpling he had ever tasted. Then, he looked at Sally Ann and licked his lips.

**Reader 1** "Uh-oh!" thought Sally Ann. "That bear is ready to eat again. And, he wants to eat **ME**!" Sally Ann thought fast. Then, she bowed. "Mr. Bear," she said, "would you please dance with me?"

**Reader 2** Sally Ann knew that all bears love to dance. It is their secret weakness. The bear bowed to Sally. As he made his bow, Sally bent down and quickly tied two long strings to his legs. Then, she started to sing. This was her song:

**"Round and round and round we go!
Dancing fast! Dancing slow!
We will dance! Oh, let us, do,
And get the chores all done, too!"**

**Reader 1** Sally Ann sang and sang. She and the bear danced and danced. They danced all around the cabin with a lively step. They danced all around the yard between the apple trees. They danced all around the fields. Then, they danced down around the pond. When they got to the woods, that bear was tired. Sally Ann danced him right up to his cave. The bear fell down on the hard ground. He was sound asleep.

**Reader 2** With one hand, Sally Ann lifted up that big old bear. She put him down on the cool floor of the cave. She patted him on the head. "I thought you would be a big problem, but you helped me out just fine!" said Sally Ann. She untied the strings from the bear's legs. Then, she went home.

**Reader 1** Now, that Sally Ann was very smart and clever. She had come up with a way to dance with the bear and get her chores done, too. She had tied one string to her churn. Every time that bear hopped up and down, he churned more butter. Sally Ann had tied the other string to her saw. Every time that bear whirled around, he sawed some wood.

**Reader 2** Sally Ann skipped happily back home to her cabin. There was a huge new stack of wood for her fire. The soft, creamy butter in the churn was all ready for supper. The stew and dumplings were cooked perfectly. Sally Ann sat down to supper and stretched out her legs. She dug into her big bowl of stew. She watched as the full moon came up over the treetops. She saw the stars start to twinkle in the dark sky.

**Reader 1** "What a fine day!" exclaimed Sally Ann. "I got a good lick of work done and no mistake."

# The Dancing Bear: Checking for Details

**Directions:** Use the vocabulary to complete the sentences.

| **Vocabulary:** | bear | bowed | cabin | cave |
|---|---|---|---|---|
| churn | dawn | dumpling | fields | licked |
| Sally Ann | weakness | whirled | | |

**1.** One day, Sally Ann had been up since _____.

**2.** She was making butter in a _____.

**3.** Sally Ann _____ into her cabin when she saw the bear.

**4.** The _____ looked at Sally Ann and _____ his lips.

**5.** Sally Ann stuffed a _____ into the bear's mouth.

**6.** Sally Ann _____ and asked Mr. Bear to dance with her.

**7.** Dancing was the bear's secret _____.

**8.** They danced around the _____ and the _____.

**9.** _____ danced the bear up to his _____.

**Directions:**
Draw a picture to show one of the ways that the bear helped Sally Ann.

Explain your picture.

Name:

# The Dancing Bear:  Thinking About the Story

**Directions:** Use sentences to answer the questions.

**1.** Think about what you read.  Illustrate to show how Sally Ann was . . .

| Fast | Powerful |
|------|----------|
|      |          |

**2.** What was Sally Ann's problem in the story?

_____

_____

**3.** How did Sally Ann show that she was smart?

_____

_____

**Try This!**  Would you like to make your own food and sew your own clothes like Sally Ann?  Explain your answer on another sheet of paper.

## – Teacher's Page –
# Davy Crockett Meets Kitten

### Prereading Activity: Science Connection

Find pictures of panthers (cougars) and read about them. How large are panthers? Why are they good hunters? How do they find their prey? Let students help you make a list of their traits.

### Demonstrating Fluent Reading

Model fluent reading for your students by reading aloud the first page. After the reading, ask students to predict what might happen next in the story.

To model a dialogue section, use Davy's words from the start of the story. Ask students, "Did you hear how I said 'No animal could ever make *ME* a-feared'? That's because Davy is talking about himself." Point out to your students that your voice got louder when you read the word *me*. This shows that Davy was boasting about how brave he was.

### Improving Vocabulary

Before students read the story, review these vocabulary words with them:

| | | | |
|---|---|---|---|
| brag | fiery | growled | manners |
| mewed | punch | glowing | hiss |

Be sure also to point out the special language of this tall tale—expressions such as "a-feared," "tarnation," and "shucks." This 19th century language is a big part of what gives tall tales their unique flavor.

### Reading with a Buddy

Pair students and have them be partners.

**Day 1:** Let students read aloud the story with "one voice" in unison to work on word recognition and fluency skills.

**Day 2:** Direct students to choose a part and read the story aloud again.

**Day 3:** Have students switch parts and reread the story to each other.

At the end of the third day, let your students show off how fluently they can read this story by taking home a copy of it. Encourage each student to read it aloud with a parent or another adult and then return the signed parent letter. (See page 6.)

### Background

The real David Crockett lived from 1786 to 1836. He had a reputation for bragging about his experiences and abilities as a woodsman. This story is based on tales of Davy Crockett's life in Tennessee. Wild animals presented a big danger for pioneers. In the Eastern woodlands, there was no fiercer hunter than the panther. That is why Davy's taming of Kitten is comforting and funny, compared to the real threat that panthers were to pioneers.

### Postreading Activities: Comprehension

**Day 1:** After they read the script aloud with partners, have the student pairs discuss what they liked about the story. You may wish to have students underline words in the story that are examples of *hyperbole*, or exaggeration.

**Day 2:** Let students complete page 40 by answering questions to recall story details.

**Day 3:** Direct students to complete the activity Thinking About the Story on page 41 by identifying hyperbole, by analyzing the main character Davy Crockett and the problem he faced, and by making an inference about Davy.

### Character Education Connection

Discuss the idea of bravery with the students.
- What does it mean to be brave?
- Is it possible to be brave and scared at the same time?
- Talk about a time that you acted bravely, even though you were scared.

# Davy Crockett Meets Kitten

**Reader 1** Davy was shaking a bit, but he knew he could not act scared. So he put his hands on his hips. "Why, look at you!" he exclaimed. "You're nothin' but a fat, little kitten!"

**Reader 2** "GRRRRR!" growled the panther.

**Reader 1** "Grrrrr yourself!" shouted Davy. "Come on down here where I can get a good look at you."

**Reader 2** The panther jumped down from the tree limb. He was the largest cat that Davy had ever seen. The panther growled again.

**Reader 1** "Hasn't anybody learned you any manners?" asked Davy.

**Reader 2** The panther stretched out his front legs. He put his head down. He was ready to jump on top of Davy!

**Reader 1** "Oh!" said Davy quickly. "So you want to race? Well, then! Come on!" And, Davy turned and started to run.

**Reader 2** The panther ran right behind him. They raced through the woods so fast that they knocked over trees. They sprinted up a hill so fast that the rocks flew up and rolled down behind them.

**Reader 1** One day, Davy Crockett was walking in the woods. He loved to brag, even when nobody could hear him. As he walked, he talked. "I am the biggest, bravest thing in these woods!" he shouted. "No animal could ever make **ME** a-feared!"

**Reader 2** "Grrrrr!" said a voice in a tree.

**Reader 1** Davy looked up and gulped. There, sitting in a nearby tree, was a panther. Now, panthers were scary. Folks called them "The Big Eaters." They were huge, tan cats with big paws and sharp claws. They had fiery eyes. They had large, sharp teeth.

**Reader 2** They quickly raced through a fast-flowing stream. All of the water splashed out of it.

**Reader 1** "Come on!" yelled Davy. "Can't you run any faster than that?"

**Reader 1** Davy could feel the hot breath of the panther on his neck. The big cat was almost on top of him. Davy stopped abruptly. The huge cat ran right into him, but Davy was ready. He quickly grabbed the animal by its tail. Then, he swung that big cat around and around over his head.

**Reader 2** The panther stopped growling. He mewed like a small cat. Davy put him down on the ground.

**Reader 1** "All right then," said Davy. "I don't want to hurt you, so don't you hurt me! You are going to come home with me. I will call you Kitten. And, I will teach you manners. You are going to be a fine cat to have as a friend."

**Reader 1** The huge panther followed Davy home to his cabin. Davy showed Kitten how to sit at the table and wait for supper with his paws folded. He showed Kitten how to use his sharp teeth to punch leather. This helped Davy to sew shirts and pants for himself. Kitten learned how to rake leaves with his huge paws. He pulled the bucket up from the well with his long tail.

**Reader 2** Kitten slept in front of the warm fire at night.

**Reader 2** This big cat had glowing eyes. At night, he could walk next to Davy in the woods and see everything. If there was danger, Kitten would stop, point with a front paw, and hiss. Then, Davy knew that it was not safe.

**Reader 2** People would call out and point when they saw Davy and Kitten walking together. "How in tarnation did you tame that big cat?" they would ask.

**Reader 1** Davy would just smile. "Shucks," he replied. "It was nothing. We just had us a little race. Then, we went home to a nice supper. Cats are good company if you know how to treat them right!"

# Davy Crockett Meets Kitten: Checking for Details

**Directions:** Answer each question with a sentence.

**1.** Where did Davy meet the panther?

_____

_____

**2.** How did Davy feel when he first saw the panther?

_____

_____

**3.** What kind of runner is Davy?

_____

**4.** What did Davy do to tame the panther? Write two of the ways.

_____

_____

**5.** Draw a picture to show one way that Kitten helped Davy. Explain your illustration.

_____

_____

_____

_____

_____

Name: _____

# Davy Crockett Meets Kitten: Thinking About the Story

**Directions:** Answer each question with a sentence.

**1.** Use words from the story. Give one example of how fast Davy and the panther ran. Illustrate a picture to show this action.

_____

_____

Why is this an exaggeration?

_____

_____

_____

**2.** What was Davy's problem in the story?

_____

_____

**3.** How does Davy feel about Kitten at the end of the story? Explain.

_____

_____

_____

**Try This!** Would you like to have a panther for a pet? Write the reasons for your answer on another sheet of paper.

# The Big Baby Ox

## Background

This story is based on the tales of Paul Bunyan's childhood. In some versions of this story, Paul is left alone in the woods by his parents and then finds the ox to comfort him.

## Demonstrating Fluent Reading

Model fluent reading for your students by reading aloud the first page. After the reading, ask students to predict what might happen next in the story.

You may wish to select portions of the text to read out loud in a choral reading. This story, like most tall tales, has amazing "facts," such as what Baby Paul ate during a day.

Model the astonishment and "build" of these lists of items. Show students how your voice rises when you add each item to emphasize the exaggeration of the details.

## Prereading Activity: Building Vocabulary

Before reading the story, review these vocabulary words with your students:

| | | | |
|---|---|---|---|
| storks | barrel | cereal | lumberjack |
| lonely | snowdrift | shivered | hoof |

## Reading with a Buddy

Pair students and have them be partners.

**Day 1:** Let students read aloud the story with "one voice" in unison to work on word recognition and fluency skills.

**Day 2:** Direct students to choose a part and read the story aloud again.

**Day 3:** Have students to switch parts and reread the story to each other.

At the end of the third day, let your students show off how fluently they can read this story by taking home a copy of it. Encourage each student to read it aloud with a parent or another adult and then return the signature sheet. (See page 6.)

## Postreading Activities: Comprehension

**Day 1:** After they read the script aloud with partners, have the student pairs discuss what they liked about the story. You may wish to have students underline words in the story that are examples of *hyperbole*, or exaggeration.

**Day 2:** Let students complete page 45 to recall details and identify cause and effect in the story.

**Day 3:** Direct students to complete the activity Thinking About the Story on page 46 by analyzing Paul Bunyan's character and the problem he faced in the woods and making an inference about Paul.

## Character Education Connection

Discuss the idea of pets.
- Have you ever had an animal as a friend? What kind of animal?
- If you could have any pet in the world, what would it be?
- Why do you think it would be hard for Paul to make friends with humans?

## Thinking Skills Connection

Imagine you had a baby the size of a house to take care of. How would you do it? What would you use to make a baby bottle? What would you use for a bed? What would you feed the baby? What would the baby wear?

# The Big Baby Ox

**Reader 1** When Paul Bunyan was a baby, he was a sight to see. It took 10 storks to get that baby to his parents. Baby Paul weighed more than 100 pounds. He didn't get to wear baby clothes. After just one week, Paul had to wear his father's pants and shirts.

**Reader 2** Feeding Paul took a lot of work. Every morning, Paul ate 20 eggs, 10 pounds of potatoes, and a barrel full of cereal. For dinner, he could eat 10 hams, 30 loaves of bread, and a tub full of salad. When he started to crawl, the ground shook. When he cried, trees fell down in the forest. Come to think of it, that is how Paul's mother and father knew he would grow up to be a lumberjack.

**Reader 1** Baby Paul did his share of work. He could catch fish. He could catch 100 fish in one day! He could plow fields. All he had to do was walk across them. His big baby feet made the field ready for planting.

**Reader 2** Paul liked to work. He liked his life. But, he was lonely. He was taller than any tree. Paul was so big it was hard for him to talk to people. He did not have a friend. "Nobody knows what it is like to be this big," thought Paul.

**Reader 1** Then one winter, there was a huge storm. This storm lasted for 10 days. It snowed and snowed. People could not open the doors to their houses. They were snowed in. The snow was not a problem for Paul. It barely came up to his knees.

**Reader 2** Paul put on his big, warm coat and his yellow scarf. He walked out in the snow. He brushed the snow away from people's houses. "Thank you, Paul!" the happy people would yell.

**Reader 1** Now, Paul was walking home through the woods, when he heard a crying sound. It sounded like this: "Ma-maaaa."

**Reader 1** "It's a baby! It's lost in the woods!" thought Paul. He called, "Where are you?"

**Reader 2** He heard the cry again. "Ma-maaaa."

**Reader 1** Paul walked all through the woods. He looked up and down. He was ready to give up. Then, he saw one ear sticking out of a snowdrift. He reached down. He pulled out a baby ox. "Ma-maaaa!" the poor ox cried.

**Reader 2** The ox was a baby, all right. But, it was the biggest baby Paul had ever seen. And the ox was blue. It had been in the cold so long that it was blue all over. It shivered. Paul lifted the ox up in his arms.

**Reader 1** "Don't worry, baby," said Paul. "I will take care of you now."

**Reader 2** Paul took the baby ox back to the farm. It was too big to walk into the barn. So Paul took the ox to his bedroom. Paul slept in a huge cave near his parents' house. He had a big, warm bed there. He set the ox down on the bed and laid down next to him. "I don't know if you will make it, baby," said Paul sadly.

**Reader 1** But by the next morning, the ox was fine. Paul woke up because the ox was licking his nose. Paul laughed so hard that many trees fell down. He had a friend at last!

**Reader 2** Paul named the blue ox Babe. Babe followed Paul like a puppy. Babe was so big each of his hoofprints made a little pond where he walked. Babe grew so fast that when Paul would blink that ox would be even bigger than he had been a second ago.

**Reader 1** When Paul grew up, he became a lumberjack. That's someone who cuts down trees. Paul loved his job. He could cut down hundreds of trees each hour.

**Reader 2** Every time Paul and Babe took a step, it was a mile. So they could cover a lot of ground in a day. Babe learned how to pull a cart to bring all of the trees back to camp. But, the best thing was that Paul had a friend. He was happy. He was never lonely again.

# The Big Baby Ox: Checking for Details

**Directions:** Use sentences to answer the questions.

Think about what you read. What did Baby Paul eat for breakfast? Illustrate a picture to show this.

Why is this an exaggeration? _____

_____

What work did Baby Paul do?

_____

_____

**Directions:** A **cause** makes something happen. An **effect** happens as a result of a cause. Draw a line from each cause to its effect.

| Cause | Effect |
|---|---|
| **1.** When Paul started to crawl, | **a.** the trees fell down. |
| **2.** At one week of age, Baby Paul was very large, | **b.** each hoofprint made a little pond. |
| **3.** When Baby Paul cried, | **c.** so he had to wear his father's pants and shirts. |
| **4.** Babe, the ox, was so large that wherever he stepped, | **d.** the ground shook. |

Name:

# The Big Baby Ox: Thinking About the Story

**Directions:** Use sentences to answer the questions.

**1.** What kind of person was Paul? Illustrate two pictures about Paul.

Tell about your pictures. _____

_____

_____

**2.** What was Paul's problem in the woods?

_____

_____

**3.** At the end of the story, why did Paul feel happy?

_____

_____

**Try This!** Why was Babe the perfect pet for Paul?
Explain your answer on another sheet of paper.

<table>
<tr><td>

**– Teacher's Page –**

# Sal and the Pirates

</td><td>

## Background
This story is based on tales of Sal Fink. Sal was the daughter of legendary keelboat operator Mike Fink.

</td></tr>
</table>

## Demonstrating Fluent Reading
Model fluent reading for your students by reading aloud the first page. After the reading, ask students to predict what might happen next in the story.

Discuss how phrasing is used to convey meaning. Ask students, "Did you hear how I grouped the words 'She started wrestling with that bolt of lightning'? That's because this is a whole thought that belongs together. Then, I paused before I read, 'And, guess who won?'"

Point out to your students how you raised your voice when you read the word *won*. Explain that is how you express the question in that sentence. Have students ask other questions to their partners and listen their voices rise as they ask them.

## Prereading Activity: Building Vocabulary
Before reading the story, review these vocabulary words with your students:

| | | | |
|---|---|---|---|
| roughest | toughest | alligator | bare |
| wrestling | bolt | lightning | pirates |

## Reading with a Buddy
Pair students and have them be partners.

**Day 1:** Let students read aloud the story with "one voice" in unison to work on word recognition and fluency skills.

**Day 2:** Direct students to choose a part and read the story aloud again.

**Day 3:** Have students switch parts and reread the story to each other.

At the end of the third day, let your students show off how fluently they can read this story by taking home a copy of it. Encourage each student to read it aloud with a parent or another adult and then return the signed parent letter. (See page 6.)

## Postreading Activities: Comprehension
**Day 1:** After they read the script aloud with partners, have the student pairs discuss what they liked about the story. You may wish to have students underline words in the story that are examples of *hyperbole*, or exaggeration.

**Day 2:** Let students complete the vocabulary and sequencing events activity on page 50.

**Day 3:** Direct students to complete the activity Thinking About the Story on page 51 by analyzing Sal Fink's character, her traits, and the problem she faced and by making an inference about Sal.

## Character Education Connection
Discuss the idea of stealing.
- Do you know somebody who lost something because it was taken from them?
- Why is stealing bad?
- How did Sal try to make up for what the pirates had stolen?

## Social Studies Connection
Look at the Mississippi River on a map. Discuss with students how this huge river was a "highway" for the country before the building of roads and railways.

## – The Tall Tale –
# Sal and the Pirates

**Reader 1** Nobody ever got the better of Sal Fink. Sal was the daughter of Mike Fink. He was the roughest, toughest boat man on the Mississippi River. But, Sal was even rougher and tougher. Why, Sal was so brave that when she was just three years old she jumped on the back of an alligator. That big old alligator swam and swam while little Sal danced on its back. She sang "Yankee Doodle Dandy" the whole time, too.

**Reader 2** Sal was so tough that she could fight a bear with her bare hands. Come to think of it, she had two little bear cubs as pets.

**Reader 1** One time, Sal saw a bolt of lightning hit the house of a friend. "You stop that!" Sal yelled. She started wrestling with that bolt of lightning. And, guess who won?

**Reader 2** Another time, Sal got into a race on her father's boat. She only had a pole to move her boat. The other boat had a big paddle wheel. And, guess who won?

**Reader 1** So most people knew to just leave Sal alone. She was fine when folks were nice. But if somebody made her mad, watch out!

**Reader 2** Too bad those old pirates didn't know that. There were 50 of them. They were bold. They went up and down the river. They took people's gold. They robbed people's houses. They stole people's boats. And the best boat on the river was owned by Mike Fink.

**Reader 1** "Aha!" said the king of the pirates. "Mike Fink has a daughter. Let's get her. We can tie her up. We can hide her. And, we'll make Mike give us his boat. Then, he can have her back."

**Reader 2** Sal was out in the woods. She was singing. Otherwise, those pirates would never have caught her—even though there were 50 of them! But, she did not know what had happened until she was all tied up.

**Reader 1** "Ha, ha!" laughed the pirate king. "Now, we will get Mike Fink's boat." Sal growled. She did not like what she heard.

**Reader 2** Sal acted like she was helpless. The pirates carried her back to their secret camp. They lit a fire. They cooked a big meal. They danced and sang. Sal sat by a tree, all tied up. She got madder and madder.

**Reader 1** Then, those silly pirates fell asleep. That was a big, big mistake. "Now then!" Sal said to herself. "Nobody is getting my pa's boat!" She had 50 ropes tied around her. But, she burst out of them like they were threads. Then, she picked up each one of those ropes. And, she used them to tie up every one of those pirates.

**Reader 2** The fire had burned down. Sal saw that the logs glowed red. "That should wake them up!" she said. One by one she tossed the pirates into the fire.

**Reader 1** "Ouch! Ooooh! Hot!" they cried. They danced around, trying to jump off the hot coals. Sal watched them and grinned.

**Reader 2** Then, she took their chest of gold. On her way home, she stopped at every house on the river. She gave every family some of the pirate gold.

**Reader 1** It was dawn when Sal got home. Her two little bear cubs ran up to greet her. She scooped them up in her arms. She went into the house. She got into bed. "Time to get a little rest," Sal told the cubs. "It's been a busy night. And tomorrow, Pa and I are going south to pick up a load of cargo!" She smiled and fell asleep.

**Reader 2** Now they say that those pirates went hopping away on their burned feet. They left the country. They never came back to the big, wild river. With Sal around, it was too wild for them!

Name: _____

## Sal and the Pirates: Checking for Details

**Directions:** Use the vocabulary to complete the sentences.

| **Vocabulary:** | 50 | asleep | boat | camp | chest |
| --- | --- | --- | --- | --- | --- |
| dawn | fire | gold | meal | pirates | river |
| ropes | threads | | | | |

Fifty bold pirates made a plan to get Mike Fink's _____ .

One day, Sal was by herself in the woods. The pirates found her and tied her up with _____. They brought her to their _____ .

Sal acted helpless as the pirates ate a big _____.
While watching them fall _____, she got madder and madder.

Just then, Sal burst out of the _____ ropes like they were _____ !

Sal worked quickly and tied up every one of the _____.

Then, she tossed the pirates into the _____ before taking their _____ of gold.

On her way home, Sal gave every family living along the _____ some of the pirates' _____.

It had been a very busy night for Sal. It was _____ when she finally got home and gave her bear cubs a hug.

**Try This!** Cut out the sentences and mix them up. Paste them in order on a sheet of paper so that they tell the story.

Name:

# Sal and the Pirates: Thinking About the Story

**Directions:** Use sentences to answer the questions.

**1.** Tell what Sal was like as a person. Use words from the story.

| How was she very tough? | How was she very brave? |
|---|---|
| How was she very strong? | How was she caring towards others? |

**2.** What was Sal's problem in the story?

_____

_____

**3.** At the end of the story, why did Sal feel happy?

_____

_____

**Try This!** If you were given a chest of gold, what would you do with it? Explain your answer on another sheet of paper.

# The Sun, the Moon, and the Stars

## Background

This story is based on Hawaiian tall tales about Kana, a stretching kupua. He is the child of Hina and a hero of many folktales. A *kupua* is a heroic trickster, one who can choose to work for good or evil.

## Reading with a Buddy

Pair students and have them be partners.

**Day 1:** Let students read aloud the story with "one voice" in unison to work on word recognition and fluency skills.

**Day 2:** Direct students to choose a part and read the story aloud again.

**Day 3:** Have students switch parts and reread the story to each other.

At the end of the third day, let your students show off how fluently they can read this story by taking home a copy of it. Encourage each student to read it aloud with a parent or another adult and then return the signed parent letter. (See page 6.)

## Postreading Activities: Comprehension

**Day 1:** After they read the script aloud with partners, have the student pairs discuss what they liked about the story. You may wish to have students underline words in the story that are examples of *hyperbole*, or exaggeration.

**Day 2:** Let students complete the activities on page 55 by recalling story details and recognizing cause and effect.

**Day 3:** Direct students to complete the activity Thinking About the Story on page 56 by analyzing the problem Kana faced and how he solved it.

## Demonstrating Fluent Reading

Model fluent reading for your students by reading aloud the first page. After the reading, ask students to predict what might happen next in the story.

Be sure to model the text (on page 54) where Kana is reaching down again and again to retrieve the treasures in the pit. Show how words such as *then* and *next* make transitions that students can hear when read aloud.

For more fluency practice, choose a fairy tale that has a repetition of tasks, such as "Goldilocks." Have your class do a choral reading of the fairy tale.

## Character Education Connection

Discuss the idea of manners.
- Why is it a good thing to be polite to people?
- Has anyone ever been rude to you? How did you feel?
- What happened when Niheu was rude to the king's man?

## Prereading Activity: Building Vocabulary

Before reading the story, review these vocabulary words with your students:

| | | | |
|---|---|---|---|
| special | poi | temper | message |
| rude | volcano | hidden | treasures |

## Social Studies Connection

Teach students about the islands of Hawaii. Talk about Hawaii's special culture and that the islands had their own kings and queens. Look at photos of island landmarks.

# – The Tall Tale –
# The Sun, the Moon, and the Stars

**Reader 1** A child was born in faraway Hawaii. He was called Kana. When he was a baby, he was sent to live with his grandmother. She felt that he was going to be a special person.

**Reader 2** Grandmother wove a mat out of vines. She put it in a hut. Then, she fed Kana for 40 days without stopping. She fed him *poi*, which is a special food made of roots. Every day the baby grew. By the end of 40 days, he was 40 feet tall.

**Reader 1** Then, Grandmother found out that Kana could grow even taller. When he needed to, he could stretch himself out. He could reach up into the sky. He could look over the clouds. When he did this, his body looked like a long, thin rope. Nobody knew why this child had such a strange gift. But, everyone knew that he was special.

**Reader 2** Kana could walk from one island in Hawaii to another in a single step. People would see a beach where rocks had fallen from a hill. Or, they would see a new little lake. They would say, "Kana has been walking here."

**Reader 1** Kana had a brother named Niheu. Niheu had a bad temper. The king sent a message to Niheu. Niheu was rude to the king's man who brought the message. That was like being rude to the king himself. The king was very angry.

**Reader 2** "I will take away the sun, the moon, and the stars!" said the king. "I will teach everyone who is boss here!"

**Reader 2** The king took the sun, the moon, and the stars out of the sky. He hid them all in a deep pit.

**Reader 1** Hawaii had been sunny and beautiful. Now, it was dark. The people were sad. They came to Grandmother. "You must help us!" they said. "Niheu made this happen. Now, he must fix it!"

**Reader 2** Grandmother said, "I do not think that Niheu can fix this. But, I think that Kana can."

**Reader 1** Kana stepped from one island to another. He looked and looked for a place where the king could hide the sun, the moon, and the stars. He took fire from a volcano to light his way.

**Reader 2** Finally, Kana found the deep pit where the sun, the moon, and the stars were hidden. He knew that he could not reach into the pit himself. The king's men would only give these treasures to the king himself.

**Reader 1** So Kana made a giant hand that looked just like the king's hand. Then, he stretched himself out until he looked like a long rope. He reached far, far down into the pit with the fake hand. "Give me my treasures," Kana called down.

**Reader 2** He pulled up the hand the first time. It was filled with all of the birds that sing when the sun comes up. Kana reached up high in the sky. He put the birds into the air.

**Reader 1** Next, he sent the hand down again. This time, the hand was filled with all of the stars from the sky. Kana stretched himself up as high as he could reach. He threw the stars back across the sky.

**Reader 2** Then, he sent the hand down and got the moon. Kana stretched until he almost snapped in half. He put the moon right back where it belonged.

**Reader 1** One more time, he sent the hand down. Up came the sun. Kana had to stretch himself so far that he was no wider than a thread. He reached and reached until he put the sun back where it had been.

**Reader 2** The next day, the sun rose again over the islands. The people of Hawaii now knew why Kana was so special.

Name: _____

# The Sun, the Moon, and the Stars: Checking for Details

**Directions:** Read each sentence about the story. Write a "**T**" on the blank if the sentence is true. Write an "**F**" on the blank if the sentence is false.

**1.** Kana ate poi for 40 days.  _____

**2.** Kana could stretch himself out to look over the clouds.  _____

**3.** Niheu was kind to the king's man.  _____

**4.** The king took the sun, moon, and stars out of the sky to show everyone who is boss.  _____

**5.** When Kana put the sun back in the sky, he was no wider than a thread.  _____

**6.** Kana found only the moon, sun, and stars in a deep pit.  _____

---

**Directions:** A **cause** makes something happen. An **effect** happens as a result of a cause. Write the cause or effect in the blank.

| Cause | Effect |
|---|---|
| **1.** _____ _____ | Kana became 40 feet tall and could stretch himself out. |
| **2.** Niheu was rude to the king's man, who brought a message. | _____ _____ |
| **3.** _____ _____ | There was no beautiful sunshine. Hawaii became dark. |

# The Sun, the Moon, and the Stars: Thinking About the Story

*Making Inferences, Analyzing*

**Directions:** Use sentences to answer the questions.

**1.** What do you think Nihue was thinking?

_____

_____

**2.** What do you think Kana was thinking?

_____

_____

**3.** What was Kana's problem in the story?

_____

_____

**4.** How was Kana able to solve the problem?

_____

_____

**Tell a Yarn About Kana!** What would be Kana's next adventure? Write your tall tale on another sheet of paper.

## – Teacher's Page –
# Stormy at Sea

## Background
This story is based on the tall tales of Albert Bulltop Stormalong. Both Massachusetts and Maine claim him as a native son.

## Demonstrating Fluent Reading
Model fluent reading for your students by reading aloud the first page. After the reading, ask students to predict what might happen next in the story.

Before having students practice certain parts of the story, remind them to watch for punctuation marks to express the thought with the right feeling. Point out the difference between a period and an exclamation point. Ask students how your voice is different when you read "I know!" from when you read, "The baby cried."

Have students look through the text, especially the dialogue, and read questions, exclamations, and declarative sentences out loud to a classmate to compare the sounds.

## Prereading Activity: Building Vocabulary
Before reading the story, review these vocabulary words with your students:

| | | | |
|---|---|---|---|
| mast | handy | octopus | forest |
| cargo | channel | slippery | foamy |

## Reading with a Buddy
Pair students and have them be partners.

**Day 1:** Let students read aloud the story with "one voice" in unison to work on word recognition and fluency skills.

**Day 2:** Direct students to choose a part and read the story aloud again.

**Day 3:** Have students switch parts and reread the story to each other.

At the end of the third day, let your students show off how fluently they can read this story by taking home a copy of it. Encourage each student to read it aloud with a parent or another adult and then return the signed parent letter. (See page 6.)

## Postreading Activities: Comprehension
**Day 1:** After they read the script aloud with partners, have the student pairs discuss what they liked about the story. You may wish to have students underline words in the story that are examples of *hyperbole*, or exaggeration.

**Day 2:** Let students complete the comprehension activity and word search on page 60.

**Day 3:** Direct students to complete the activity Thinking About the Story on page 61 by identifying exaggeration, analyzing the problem Stormy faced, and by making an inference about him.

## Character Education Connection
Discuss the idea of belonging or fitting in.
- Why are some people happy in one place and not in another?
- Why do you think Stormy always wanted to be at sea?

## Science Connection
Talk about storms. Why are places along the oceans especially in danger from some kinds of storms? Show pictures of hurricanes and tidal waves.

# – The Tall Tale –
# Stormy at Sea

**Reader 1** Long ago, there was a huge storm. A giant wave crashed over the houses at Cape Cod. The storm ended after 10 days. The wave had washed something onto the beach. It was the biggest baby anyone had ever seen.

**Reader 2** The baby cried. It wanted food. It drank 100 barrels of milk. While the baby was drinking his milk, the people of Cape Cod talked. They said, "We will name this baby Stormalong because he came from the storm." But soon, they all called him Stormy.

**Reader 1** Stormy was happy when he was at sea. He swam with the whales. He could swim far out to sea in just a few hours. That was because he was so big. By the time Stormy was 10 years old, he was 35 feet tall.

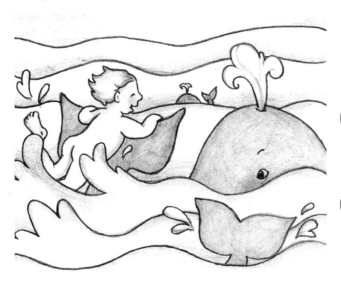

**Reader 2** Stormy worked on a ship. But it was hard to have Stormy on board. He took up so much room! The sailors had to sleep in the masts. But, he was a hard worker. He was also handy to have around. One time, his ship just stopped moving. Stormy dove into the sea. He found a big octopus hanging onto the ship. It would not let go—at least, not until it saw Stormy.

**Reader 1** The people of Cape Cod wanted to help Stormy. They held a big meeting. "Maybe he could go to Boston," said one person. "It's a much bigger place than here."

**Reader 2** "He would not like it there," said someone else. "He needs to be at sea."

**Reader 1** "I know!" shouted a third person. "We could build him a boat. Stormy needs a boat that is big enough for him to sail."

**Reader 2** "Hooray!" shouted all the people. They were the best boat builders in the world.

**Reader 1** The people of Cape Cod built Stormy a boat. It was the biggest sailing ship in the world. It was called the *Courser*. The sail makers had to go out west to the desert to spread out the sails and sew them. The mast makers had to go north to the forest to get 200-year-old trees for the masts. Finally one day, the ship was done.

**Reader 2** "Now, I can go all over the world!" said Stormy. He started to take cargo from one place to another. Stormy could climb the *Courser*'s mast and see all the way to the land across the sea. That made it easy for him to steer the ship.

**Reader 1** Now one time Stormy wanted to sail through the English Channel. That is a waterway between England and France. When the crew saw the channel, they knew the ship was in trouble. It was too big! "We will get stuck!" they cried to Stormy.

**Reader 2** But, Stormy was calm. "Just get all of the soap we have on board," he said. The sailors carried up buckets and buckets of soap. "Pour it over the sides of the ship!" said Stormy. That made the *Courser* slippery. That ship slipped right through the channel. But it left the waves all foamy and white. They are still that way today.

**Reader 1** Everyone talked about Stormy. Every sailor had stories about the great ship captain. They said that he wore a coat made of sails. They said he ate fish eggs for breakfast, fish soup for lunch, and fish stew for supper. They said that if his ship ever got stuck on sandbars, he lifted it up with one hand and kept on going.

**Reader 2** Stormy was very happy at sea. Only the sea was big enough for him. He went swimming every day with the whales. And every night, he climbed the huge mast to look at the stars.

Name:

## Stormy at Sea:  Checking for Details

**Directions:** Read each sentence about the story.  Write a "**T**" on the blank if the sentence is true.  Write an "**F**" on the blank if the sentence is false.

**1.** Stormy's ship was called the *Mouser*.  _____

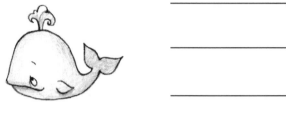

**2.** Stormy liked to swim with the whales.  _____

**3.** Stormy worked alone on his ship.  _____

**4.** The people of Boston built Stormy a ship.  _____

**5.** The crew poured buckets of soap over the sides of the
ship so that it could slide through the English Channel.  _____

**6.** The sail makers had to work in the desert to sew the sails
for Stormy's new ship.  _____

**7.** If his boat got stuck on a sandbar, Stormy would lift it up
with one hand.  _____

**Directions:** Read the words in the Word Bank.  Circle them in the word find.

**Word Bank**

baby
beach
boat
cargo
crew
forest
handy
mast
octopus
slippery
waterway
whales

| t | o | c | t | o | p | u | s |
|---|---|---|---|---|---|---|---|
| d | b | e | a | c | h | l | h |
| c | w | h | a | l | e | s | a |
| r | p | r | t | f | t | s | n |
| e | b | g | l | o | a | c | d |
| w | a | t | e | r | w | a | y |
| e | b | u | q | e | w | r | x |
| d | y | m | a | s | t | g | z |
| b | b | o | a | t | q | o | w |
| s | l | i | p | p | e | r | y |

Name:

# Stormy at Sea: Thinking About the Story

**Directions:** Use sentences to answer the questions.

**1.** Think about what you read. Illustrate a picture to show Stormy's boat.

Why were the sails sewn in the desert?

_____

_____

_____

**2.** What words did the author use to tell you about the size of the masts?

_____

_____

**3.** What was Stormy's problem as captain of his ship?

_____

_____

**4.** Why did Stormy like being at sea instead of on land?

_____

_____

**Tell a Yarn About Stormy!** What would be Stormy's next adventure? Write your tall tale on paper.

# Answer Key

**Johnny Appleseed and the Animals**................... **10**
Across
2. wolf, 4. pot, 7. earth, 8. shoes, 11. settlers, 12. cider, 13. stones

Down
1. apples, 3. limped, 5. post, 6. ghost, 9. horse, 10. sacks, 11. seeds

**Johnny Appleseed and the Animals**................... **11**
Cause and Effect
1. b. The seeds were good for planting and Johnny gave them away to people.
2. b. The wolf followed Johnny like a huge dog.
3. a. Johnny planted apple trees everywhere he went.

Bottom section
1. The wolf's leg was caught in a big, steel trap. Johnny had to help the wolf by setting it free and then caring for its injured leg.
2. Answers will vary. Johnny cared about animals which he showed by helping them. His gentle care helped Jenny the horse feel better, and he freed and cared for the wolf.

**Bess Call** ................................................ **15**
Bess: won the match, tied a horseshoe into a knot, lived on a farm
The stranger: lost the match, traveled far, laughed at the other person
Both: liked to wrestle, wanted to win

**Bess Call** ................................................ **16**
1. Answers will vary.
2. Answers will vary.
3. She needed to wrestle the stranger so that he would leave her and her brother alone.
4. Answers will vary. Joe felt relieved that he didn't have to wrestle the stranger. He was tired of wrestling others.

**Annie and the Storm** ............................... **20**
1. T, 2. F, 3. T, 4. F, 5. T, 6. T, 7. F

Word Find

| c | t | p | o | u | n | d | s |
|---|---|---|---|---|---|---|---|
| a | w | a | i | s | t | h | x |
| p | z | o | v | t | c | o | j |
| t | x | b | w | o | r | t | u |
| a | b | a | h | r | a | e | m |
| i | s | r | e | m | i | l | p |
| n | t | r | e | t | n | v | w |
| k | e | e | l | b | o | a | t |
| d | e | l | q | b | w | o | l |
| q | r | s | p | d | o | c | k |

**Annie and the Storm** ............................... **21**
1. Words underlined: Annie could steer her boat all by herself. She could carry things on and off all by herself. In fact, she could carry three barrels at the same times—one under each arm and one on her head. Exaggeration: No person is able to carry three barrels at the same time.
2. The riverboat captain would not let Annie steer in the storm. The passengers needed to leave the boat because it could possibly sink.
3. Answers may vary. Annie was feeling very confident about getting the people home safely.

**Widowmaker**......................................... **25**
Across
3. stamped, 5. lasso, 7. coyote, 9. range, 10. ranch

Down
1. Widowmaker, 2. cactus, 3. swing, 4. horse, 6. rode, 7. cowboy, 8. Texas

**Widowmaker**......................................... **26**
1. Bill could rope anything you told him to. He could rope a cactus, a whole barn, and a tornado. Exaggeration: A person is not able to rope a barn or tornado.
2. Bill chose Widowmaker as his horse, but Widowmaker didn't like to be ridden.
3. Bill promised Widowmaker that no one else was allowed to ride him. Bill also gave Widowmaker food, water, and attention.

**Pecos Bill Gets Married** ......................... **30**
One day, Bill was riding Widowmaker along the Pecos River. In the water was the biggest catfish Bill had ever seen. And, riding on the back of the fish was Slue-Foot Sue. That night, Bill thought about Sue. He howled like a coyote at the moon. Sue agreed to marry Bill if she could ride Widowmaker. After the wedding, Sue put a saddle on the horse and then jumped on his back. Widowmaker bucked so hard that Sue flew over the moon. Using his lasso, Bill roped Sue to get her back again. Sue told Bill about the water in the Big Dipper. So he roped it to bring rain to Texas.

**Pecos Bill Gets Married** ......................... **31**
1. Slue-Foot Sue could ride a giant catfish. Exaggeration: Catfish do not grow to be huge. No person can ride a real catfish.
2. Bill wanted to marry Sue, but she would only agree to it if she could ride Widowmaker. Bill has promised Widowmaker that no one else would ride him.
3. Snakes fainted. Hens laid fried eggs. Sheep turned into balls of dust.
4. Answers may vary. Bill probably felt very happy and satisfied that he could help people by bringing rain to Texas.

# Correlations to NCTE/IRA Standards and NAEYC/IRA Position Statement

*Partner Read-Alouds: Tall Tales* supports the National Council of Teachers of English (NCTE) and International Reading Association (IRA) *Standards for the English Language Arts.* This resource also supports the following recommendations from *Learning to Read and Write: Developmentally Appropriate Practices for Young Children,* a position statement of the National Association for the Education of Young Children (NAEYC) and the International Reading Association (IRA).

## NCTE/IRA *Standards for the English Language Arts*

Each activity in this book supports one or more of the following standards:

1. **Students read many different types of print and nonprint texts for a variety of purposes.**
   Students read tall tales plus worksheets related to them while doing the activities in this book.

2. **Students read literature from various time periods, cultures, and genres in order to form an understanding of humanity.**
   The reading passages in *Partner Read-Alouds: Tall Tales* are based on classic American tall tales. This book also offers additional literature suggestions, such as fairy tales and picture books.

3. **Students use a variety of strategies to build meaning while reading.**
   Activities in this book support strategies and skills essential to effective reading, such as read aloud with expression and understanding, recall details, sequence events, recognize cause and effect, identify the main character's problem and solution, compare and contrast characters' traits, and make inferences.

4. **Students communicate in spoken, written, and visual form, for a variety of purposes and a variety of audiences.**
   Students speak during partner read-alouds, class discussions, and performances; write words, sentences, and paragraphs; and draw while doing the activities in *Partner Read-Alouds: Tall Tales.*

5. **Students use the writing process to write for different purposes and different audiences.**
   Students use parts of the writing process such as prewriting while they write sentences, paragraphs, and tall tales in this book.

6. **Students incorporate knowledge of language conventions (grammar, spelling, punctuation), media techniques, and genre to create and discuss a variety of print and nonprint texts.**
   While talking about the stories in this resource book and writing their own tall tales, students analyze the characteristics of this genre and note how punctuation affects oral expression and the meaning of the text.

7. **Students begin to understand and respect the diversity of language across cultures, regions, ethnicities, and social roles.**
   *Partner Read-Alouds: Tall Tales* introduces students to the hyperbole and era-specific language used in traditional tall tales.

8. **Students become participating members of a variety of literacy communities.**
   The partner read-alouds, group discussions, and performances in this book help teachers build a classroom literacy community.

## NAEYC/IRA Position Statement *Learning to Read and Write: Developmentally Appropriate Practices for Young Children*

The activities in this book support the following recommended teaching practices for primary-grade students:

1. **Teachers read to children daily and provide opportunities for students to read independently both fiction and nonfiction texts.**
   Teachers model reading tall tales fluently to students and give them the opportunity to read the stories aloud with a partner and to family members. Students also read worksheets to do the activities in this book.

2. **Teachers provide opportunities for students to write many different kinds of texts for different purposes.**
   Students write words, sentences, paragraphs, and tall tales while doing the activities in *Partner Read-Alouds: Tall Tales.*

3. **Teachers provide opportunities for children to work in small groups.**
   Students work in small groups by reading the tall tale out loud with a partner.

4. **Teachers provide challenging instruction that expands children's knowledge of their world and expands vocabulary.**
   *Partner Read-Alouds: Tall Tales* expands student vocabulary by presenting story-specific vocabulary along with period-specific words and figurative language used in tall tales.